MW00378511

THE SECRET PLACE

THE SECRET PLACE

HOW TO ENTER THE SPIRITUAL PLACE OF SAFETY AND REST

THE GATES OF HULDAH

Copyright © June 12, 2022 Gates of Huldah

All rights reserved. "No part of this book may be reproduced, distributed, or transmitted in any form or by any means, including photocopying, recording, or other electronic or mechanical methods, or by any information storage and retrieval system without the prior written permission of the publisher, except in the case of very brief quotations embodied in critical reviews and certain other noncommercial uses permitted by copyright law."

The Secret Place

For permissions, contact Gates of Huldah
contact@gatesofhuldah.com

Contents

INTRODUCTION

In this book, we will study the verses loved by many that are found in Psalm 91. This passage of Scripture is a favorite for several believers because it expresses the idea of having the Most High's protection and deliverance from danger. I was moved to write this book to help those who have a desire to pray more effectively. Our time of prayer is precious. It is a time to commune with the Creator of everything that is. It is also a powerful weapon for those who believe in Him and have a yearning to develop a more robust prayer life. Understanding the mysteries of the "secret place" will support you on this quest to take your prayer life to higher heights. The mentor text used in this endeavor will be the 91st chapter of the Book of Psalm.

The first verse of Psalm 91 begins by using the earliest names for God - "Most High" (El-Elyon) and "Almighty" (Shaddai).

He who dwells in the secret place of the Most High shall abide under the shadow of the Almighty (Psalm 91:1 NKJV).

We see these two names used for the Creator: Most High and Almighty. Namely, you are to understand that there is no one greater and you are to understand that there is no one more powerful. By calling Himself Most High, the message is clear that there is no one or anything higher than the Creator of heaven and earth. As Most High, He reigns supreme. By referring to Him as Almighty, it leaves no room for doubt that there is none more powerful or stronger.

In addition, the Almighty is the Supreme ruler. He is referred to by many names. The name of the God of the Israelites was revealed to Moses as four Hebrew consonants YHWH, called the Tetragrammaton. The name is also shown in Psalm 68:4 as YAH. We call His name whenever we say, hallelujah, which many believe to be the highest praise. Praise ye YAH is the declaration made when we offer up this praise (The Editors of Encyclopaedia Britannica).

> *Sing to God, sing praises to His name; extol Him who rides on the clouds, by His name YAH, and rejoice before Him (Psalm 68:4 NKJV).*

If we are to enter into a personal relationship with the Most High, it is only fitting that we call Him by His true name. It is the name higher than any other. So, throughout the book, I will also refer to the Highest as YAH.

Chapter 1

WHAT IS THE SECRET PLACE?

Curiosity will compel many to want to know what the secret place is and then to know why it is a secret. The phrase secret place is found in the Old and New Testament books of the Bible. Defined in its simplest term, the secret place is a place of safety for those who put their trust in the Almighty. Psalm 27:5 equates the secret place with a shelter where one would go to hide in the time of trouble. Psalm 31:20 describes it as a covering of the presence of YAH for those seeking shelter from their enemies. Another definition can be found in Psalm 17:8 for this place. Here we find that the secret place is a hiding place under the wings of the Most High. There are other descriptors throughout the Scriptures that give us insight into what the secret place is, but it is clear that it is a place of hiding.

The first verse of Psalm 91 speaks of the secret place of the Highest. "Secret place" is in Hebrew, Strong's H5643, cether, from the three-letter primitive root H5641, cather. Cether is synonymous with a hiding place, a covert in a mountain, a veil or covering, a protection, a defense, or a private or clandestine place.

Believers see this psalm as a source of comfort and protection in times of suffering, which has caused it to be known as the Soldier's Psalm or Soldier's Prayer. There is a story that tells of a military

Brigade commander in WWI who gave his soldiers a card with the passage from Psalm 91 printed on it. It just so happens that the number of the Brigade had the same number – 91st Brigade. The soldiers agreed to recite the passage daily. It is said that after the men began praying the prayer, they fought three of the bloodiest battles in WWI, yet the brigade suffered no casualties in combat while other brigades experienced as much as 90 percent. Whether this story is true or not, it shows that there is a high degree of fascination with this psalm, and many consider it a favorite prayer of protection (Homan).

As we continue to unpack the verses in Psalm 91, we will see that the secret place is also a location in the spirit realm where one can fellowship with the Creator. It serves as a refuge from the attacks of enemies. There is no one with enough power or authority to challenge those covered by YAH when they are in this place. It is also safe to say that when one enters this alcove, he comes under His protection. This is significant because it assures us that we are protected by the most powerful force there is. The realization that there is nothing that can come against us when we are under the protection of the Almighty brings comfort and joy.

Psalm 27:5 says, *"For He will hide me in His shelter in the day of trouble; He will conceal me under the cover of His tent; He will lift me high upon a rock."* The word shelter is the word "cether" in Hebrew referring to a place where you can go to hide or be concealed from your enemies.

We can see from this verse that the secret place is a spiritual hiding place. But what are hiding places used for? A hiding place is a specific place. It is not random. It is a place selected beforehand, much like a bunker. This location has been identified by you and selected as the place where you would go for protection. It is also appropriate to think about who would need to use a secret place. People who need protection and those who want to stay safe from impending danger would certainly benefit from having a secret place. It is beneficial to have a place to hide or conceal things considered most precious.

Verse 2 of Psalm 91 tells us that we are safe in the secret place. I will say of the Lord, "He is my refuge and my fortress; My God, in Him I will trust."

The metaphors describing the Highest as a refuge and fortress assure the believer that when he enters a place that is fortified and protected, he is shielded from anything that can possibly harm him. When we think of fortresses, we imagine a well-fortified place, much like a military stronghold or prison with defenses all around to keep intruders out. While thinking about prison, it may be easy to imagine tall buildings with high walls or barbed wire fences enclosing them. Undoubtedly, the facility would also have detection systems and armed guards patrolling the perimeter. Of course, the main purpose of this type of security is to thwart inmates from escaping. However, the secret place described in Psalm 91 is just the opposite. Its protective measures protect those who enter in. There can be no safer place than to seek shelter in this place where the Almighty dwells. An enemy would have to defeat Him first to harm you. His name has already indicated that there is no one capable of defeating Him, so the believer can rest secure. When we enter the secret place, we can rest and draw strength from Him.

As we consider the times ahead, the children of the Highest should take comfort in realizing that we will have shelter in the time of storm. Knowing that there is no enemy more powerful than the Most High makes the secret place a guaranteed place of maximum security. This type of protection is reserved for all who will put their hope in the God of creation.

Why is it Secret?

Now that we know what the secret place is, it is just as important to know why it is secret. Secrecy is the practice of hiding information from certain individuals or groups who do not have the "need to know", perhaps while sharing it with select individuals. That which is kept hidden is known as the secret. Secretive things are not known, seen nor is it meant to be known or seen by everyone. When you are in the know about things that are kept from others, it is easy to cultivate an air of importance. This may cause you to stand a little taller and stick your chest out a bit more because you know the secret.

There are many who will never enter this next level of intimacy with the Most High. They have been taught that prayer is just a time to pull out a book of repetitive words designed for you to say at a set time each day. Messiah admonishes us in Matthew 6 to avoid such practices.

> **And when you pray, do not use vain repetitions as the heathen do. For they think that they will be heard for their many words (Matthew 6:7 NKJV).**

Yet there are others who will not enter this realm because their relationship with YAH is superficial. They are religious with no true relationship with Elohim. They wear religion like a piece of clothing that can be tossed aside when it is not needed. This person is much like the Pharisee mentioned in Luke 18:13. He was prideful and self-righteous.

> *The Pharisee stood and prayed thus with himself, 'God, I thank You that I am not like other men—extortioners, unjust, adulterers, or even as this tax collector. 12 I fast twice a week; I give tithes of all that I possess.' 13 And the tax collector, standing afar off, would not so much as raise his eyes to heaven, but beat his breast, saying, 'God, be merciful to me a sinner!' (Luke 18:11-13 NKJV).*

This man was confident in his own righteousness. He believed that he deserved to gain access to the presence of the Highest because of his works, as indicated by his statement of the number of times he fasted and the amount of money he gave. If we were to consider the things, he pointed out as proof of his righteousness, by all accounts, he would be commended in the eyes of men. The Pharisee pointed out that he was not an extortioner or unjust. His list of good deeds included avoiding adultery, fasting and being a tither. These are all good things, but our good works will not exonerate us before the King. Did he make the outside of the cup clean and ignore the filthiness on the inside of the cup? Isaiah puts it into the proper perspective for us.

> *But we are all like an unclean thing, and all our righteousnesses are like filthy rags; we all fade as a leaf, and our iniquities, like the wind, have taken us away (Isaiah 64:6 NKJV).*

From the verses, above it should be clear that to enter the secret place, we must humble ourselves and acknowledge that we can never make ourselves good enough or be pure enough on our own merits. YAH raises us up when we lower ourselves before Him. We have been given a conscience to convict us of sin. Do not ignore the subtle tugging in our heart prompting us to deal with secret sins. When your heart is not right in the sight of the King, you cannot enter His presence until you acknowledge the sin and repent. Make the inside of the cup clean so that He can fill it with His Spirit.

Chapter 2

WHERE IS THE SECRET PLACE?

Does the secret place exist in the natural realm or is it strictly supernatural? This secret place is the place where we meet with the Almighty one-on-one. A natural location may be used to connect with the Father, like the prayer closet mentioned by Messiah in Matthew 6. However, the experience happens in the spirit realm. Consider your heart as the door, portal, or access point. Just like the heart is considered a physical organ within the body, you also have a spiritual heart. It is unseen in the natural, but the Scriptures refer to it often. It is the seat of man. Our emotions and desires begin in our heart. It pushes the will of man towards action as we see in the verse below.

> *Let us draw near with a true heart in full assurance of faith, having our hearts sprinkled from an evil conscience and our bodies washed with pure water (Hebrews 10:22 NKJV)*

Jeremiah 17:9 also tells us that the heart is deceitful and wicked above all things. When we consider these words, it would be impossible to strictly label the heart as an organ only existing in the natural because we know that our physical hearts help us to live. The physical heart is an organ that pumps blood. Yet, we also have a spiritual place in the deep recesses of our being called the heart where our Maker tabernacles and communes with us. His Spirit connects with our spirit there and allows deep to calls out to deep. It is here where the Spirit of YAH encourages, teaches, strengthens, and guides us.

The Hill of the LORD

There is another location associated with the secret place. In Scripture, it is called the Hill of the LORD in the Old Testament. The name of this place was Naioth, a biblical place located in Ramah. According to Bible Atlas, this ancient city in the land of Israel was located in the territory belonging to the tribe of Benjamin, whose name means "height" (Bible Atlas: Ramah, accessed 25 November 2016). It is represented as a place where the prophets dwelt together.

Naioth was also the home of Samuel's parents, Elkanah and Hannah. Naioth is mentioned in 1 Samuel 19:18-19 and again in 1 Samuel 19:22-23. Naioth was the home of a group of prophets over which Samuel presided. Another word used for Naioth is Navith; meaning the abode of the prophets according to Strong's Concordance #5121.

Before Saul was anointed king of Israel, he was sent by Samuel to the place called the "hill of God" in Ramah as referenced in 1 Samuel 10:5. Samuel told him that he would meet a group of prophets coming down from the high place and the Spirit of the LORD would come upon him and that he would prophesy. When Saul got there, things happened exactly as Samuel had prophesied. Saul did indeed meet prophets coming down from the "high place," and he too started to prophesy, and the passage says that he turned into another man.

The story of Saul's experience in this place gives us insight into a hallowed space that has been dedicated to the Almighty. Just going to that location causes one to have a supernatural experience due to the presence of the Highest that remained. To get into this place, you must enter it physically, but your encounter is beyond anything that we can experience naturally. The owner of this place is the Most High. His presence dwells there. When you enter this space, you come under something – His shadow. His presence overshadows you. It should be our desire to dwell continuously in this place. "Dwells" in Hebrew is Strong's H3427, yashab, "to sit, to sit down, to remain or abide, to dwell in or inhabit." The root, יָשַׁב, is the yod + shin + bet. It is here where you come in and have a seat. You are at rest ('H3427 - Yāšaḇ - Strong's Hebrew Lexicon (Kjv)').

Later, we find that Samuel and David took refuge together in Naioth to escape from the wrath of Saul after he became king. Tormented by an evil spirit, Saul pursued David mercilessly in his attempt to kill the future king. David's divine deliverance at Naioth can be found in the book of 1 Samuel 19. On approaching Naioth in pursuit of David, Saul was overcome by the Spirit of Elohim once again, he was affected supernaturally by the Spirit of the Most High and began to prophesy," causing people to ask, "Is Saul also among the prophets?" Saul's intent was to come to this place to kill David, but the presence of YAH was so intense in this place that it caused him to lay prostrate all day and night. The presence of YHWH overpowered him and caused him to worship instead. David's enemy was made to be at peace with him in the secret place. The Spirit of

YAH weakened Saul. Meanwhile, David was able to escape ('Bible Map: Naioth (Mizpah 3)').

> **He who dwells in the secret place of the Highest shall abide under the shadow of the Almighty (Psalm 91:1).**

We see that protection comes to those who dwell in this place. There is no need to fear anything that could harm us. Your enemies will have to be at peace with you when you enter this place.

The third and fourth verses of Psalm 91 provide a beautiful example of how YAH provides a protective barrier around His people. An example of this is how David was protected as he was being hunted like a wild animal. The third verse speaks of a fowler. A fowler is a hunter of birds. Saul was not hunting birds. He was hunting David. He wanted to destroy any future hopes of a Davidic kingdom. When David fled to Ramah, he entered the protective zone. He escaped the trap of the hunter determined to kill him. Considering this story, the Hill of the LORD is surely a fortress for the children of the Most High, as described in Psalm 91:3-4.

> **³ Surely He shall deliver you from the snare of the fowler and from the perilous pestilence.4 He shall cover you with His feathers, and under His wings you shall take refuge; His truth shall be your shield and buckler (Psalm 91:3-4).**

These verses are such a lovely depiction of the strength of our protector. If we were to imagine an eagle sheltering her eaglets with her strong wings to protect them from predators and any harmful thing, it would give us a good idea of how our Father hides us from danger. As the verse says, He shall cover us with His feathers and under His wings, He allows us to take refuge. This scene is describing a sanctuary where the Creator serves as a shield of protection for His people.

We find in Psalm 35:2 that David asks the LORD to take up His shield and buckler and come to his defense.

> **Take hold of shield and buckler and stand up for my help (Psalm 35:2).**

David prayed for a shield and buckler. What is the difference between the two? A buckler is a small shield that is much lighter. The Jewish Encyclopedia provides the below definition:

The Israelites used two kinds of shields—a large one that covered the whole body and was carried by the heavy-armed infantry, and a small, easily managed one, carried by the light-armed troops. The former was called "ẓinnah"; it served to protect the spearmen. Prominent warriors and leaders had their shields carried before them by special bearers. The small shield was called "magen," and was carried by the bowmen and light troops, as well as by the king (Hirsch and Benzinger).

Psalm 91:4 lets us know that truth serves as a shield and buckler. The Word of Elohim defends and protects. Do not miss the point that the Word of YAH is a weapon to destroy an enemy as well as the armor used to keep you safe from the weapons used by an enemy. Hallelujah!

Not only will the Almighty protect us from those who seek to destroy our lives. He will also keep us safe from frightful things coming against us while we sleep and plagues.

> *5 You shall not be afraid of the terror by night, Nor of the arrow that flies by day,*
> *6 Nor of the pestilence that walks in darkness, Nor of the destruction that lays waste at noonday (Psalm 91:5-6 NKJV).*

This protection is greater than any vaccine modern science can create against a plague or infectious disease. The verses above also serve as words of comfort to know that we can be protected from harmful diseases and epidemics. There is no greater assurance than to know that we can turn to our Father in heaven to keep us safe from plagues and viruses that can bring nations around the world to a halt.

The following verses go on to say that you may be standing amid thousands who are dying from the effects of pestilence and destruction, but it will not come near you. This is like what Shadrach, Meshach and Abednego experienced when Nebuchadnezzar commanded that they be thrown in the fire. Those who were following the orders of the king were burned up instead.

> *7 A thousand may fall at your side, And ten thousand at your right hand; But it shall not come near you.*
> *8 Only with your eyes shall you look, And see the reward of the wicked (Psalm 91:7-8 NKJV).*

We can take comfort in the protection that the Almighty gives to those who trust Him. We also find these reassuring words for demonic spirits that would try to attack us during the night.

In peace I will lie down and sleep, for you alone, LORD, make me dwell in safety (Psalm 4:8 NKJV).
When you lie down, you will not be afraid; when you lie down, your sleep will be sweet (Proverbs 3:24 NIV).

Many imagine the terror by night to be terrifying dreams. Job describes an experience that caused him to fear during the night. His experience was so terrifying that it caused the hair on his body to stand on end.

> [13] *Amid disquieting dreams in the night, when deep sleep falls on people,*
> [14] *fear and trembling seized me and made all my bones shake.*
> [15] *A spirit glided past my face, and the hair on my body stood on end.*
> [16] *It stopped, but I could not tell what it was. A form stood before my eyes, and I heard a hushed voice (Job 4:13-16 NIV).*

Whatever is causing distress, YAH's faithfulness to His promises will be a defense against all hostile forces. His children have no need to fear. Our Most High covers, protects and delivers those who will put their trust in Him.

Chapter 3

PROTECTION IN THE SECRET PLACE

We don't have to look far to find news about disasters and other maladies in the world. There is a constant bombardment of information coming across the various media outlets every day to let us know that we are living in perilous times, but for the people of the Most High, there is divine protection in the secret place. The verses from Psalm 91 are clear as to why this protection happens. This protection is not happenstance. His people are protected because they made Him their refuge. The children of Yah have a part to play. They must trust Him! There are assurances that come from being a child of the Creator of the universe. Regardless of the dangers seen and unseen, Messiah said that He will never leave or forsake His people. That is good news particularly now that the days are getting darker and darker. These are all signs pointing to the end of the age. There is no need to fear.

As we continue to read, we find comfort in the verse that says a thousand may fall at your side and ten thousand at your right hand. This means that even though we are greatly outnumbered by the wicked, verses 9 through 13 tell us no evil shall befall us. The verses provide us with a promise of protection from plagues and other forms of danger. The most important point is that we receive this protection because we made the Most High our dwelling place. A dwelling place is a place where someone lives. It is not a place that you visit periodically. No. The place where you dwell is your home. This is the place where you find refuge and shelter from danger.

> *⁹ Because you have made the Lord, who is my refuge,*
> *Even the Most High, your dwelling place,*
> *¹⁰ No evil shall befall you,*
> *Nor shall any plague come near your dwelling;*
> *¹¹ For He shall give His angels charge over you,*
> *To keep you in all your ways.*
> *¹² In their hands they shall bear you up,*
> *Lest you dash your foot against a stone.*
> *¹³ You shall tread upon the lion and the cobra,*
> *The young lion and the serpent you shall trample underfoot*
> *(NKJV).*

Would the Most High give a guarantee that no evil will befall us in the secret place if this is not true? We know from His word that He is not a man that He should lie, so these passages are a source of comfort. Notice that this protection extends to our home. Verse 10 says no evil can come near our dwelling because YAH's angels are instructed to stand guard and not let anything happen to us. This is an amazing promise to those who will put their trust in Him.

As we draw closer to the time of the Messiah's return, we can expect to see things that will cause many to fear. In Luke 21, He told His disciples that terrible things would happen to cause men's hearts to fail. It may be hard to imagine how horrendous the events will be, but in spite of it all, we can turn to our Father and King and know that we will be safe because we honor Him and love Him.

Fathers desire to protect their children and keep them safe from dangerous situations. Is it surprising to us that the Almighty would do the same? Listen to what the verses below are saying to us.

> [14] *"Because he has set his love upon Me, therefore I will deliver him; I will set him on high, because he has known My name" (NKJV).*

The Father takes note of those who love Him. He says He will deliver you because you set your love upon Him and because you know His name. Knowing His name is extremely important. How amazing it is to know that you will be set on high because you know His name. He goes on to say that He will answer those who call upon Him. You are not calling Him by the name of idols and pagan gods. You call upon the name of the one true God.

The added blessings from the verses in Psalm 91 are not only will you be delivered in time of trouble but that you will also be rewarded with honor and long life. These amazing promises demonstrate the goodness of our heavenly Father. He wants to do good for those who love Him. He says that He will show you His salvation. Salvation is deliverance from whatever may be trying to destroy you.

> [15] *He shall call upon Me, and I will answer him; I will be with him in trouble; I will deliver him and honor him.*
> [16] *With long life I will satisfy him, And show him My salvation." (Psalm 91:15-16).*

In Exodus 24, we read how God called Moses, Aaron, his sons and 70 elders to come up to Mount Sinai and worship Him. The glory of Elohim served as a covering for them. In Exodus 24:11 it says that they ate, drank and fellowshipped with Elohim.

There "they saw God, and they ate and drank".

But after this, we see in Exodus 24:15 that Moses was told to come up near YHVH alone.

"Then Moses went up into the mountain, and a cloud covered the mountain. Now the glory of the LORD rested on Mount Sinai, and the cloud covered it six days. And on the seventh day He called to Moses out of the midst of the cloud. The sight of the glory of the LORD was like a consuming fire on the top of the mountain in the eyes of the children of Israel."(Exodus 24:15-17).

This had to be an amazing experience for Moses. But notice that Moses had to wait six days in the clouds before going into the presence of the Highest. He went in on the seventh day. The Most High told Moses when to come near. He set the time. We may refer to Moses' time of waiting as a time of consecration or purification. After the seven days, Moses met with YHVH face to face and received the commandments. Moses enjoyed communion and conversation with the Creator of all things that exist. We can experience this time of fellowship with our Father as well. During our time of prayer, we should expect Him to speak. Oftentimes, when we pray, we talk and leave before the Father ever has a chance to respond. We should take delight in having Him speak to us. During this special time of communing with Him, we can bask in His presence, be protected, and experience His glory. This is the place where the glory of Elohim dwells.

In Exodus 24:17, the glory was described as devouring fire. Can you imagine what this was like for Moses? This experience was like nothing he had ever experienced before. To be surrounded by a presence that looks like devouring fire would certainly keep an enemy at bay. Thankfully, Moses had nothing to fear. The Scriptures tell us that he remained there for forty days and forty nights. He did not have to worry about harm from his enemies, and he had no need for natural food or drink. He was sustained as he communed with YHVH.

Fellowshipping with His creation appears to be very important to Elohim. The Bible begins and ends with Him connecting with His creation. In Genesis, it says that He would often spend time with Adam in the Garden of Eden. He came to where Adam dwelled to commune with him. Also, in the book of Revelation, Eden returns to earth where the people of the Most High can once again enjoy his presence in the place where we will dwell. At the heart of it all is relationship—one on one time with the One who made us. "I will dwell among the people of Israel and be their God. And they shall know that I am the Lord their God, who brought them out of the land of Egypt that I might dwell among them" (Ex 29:45-46).

Scripture makes it clear that all of life is about being in YAH's presence. It is there that we find peace, joy and His protection.

Chapter 4

HOW DO WE ENTER THE SECRET PLACE?

To come under YAH's protection, one way would be to enter His presence in the secret place. Another way is to invoke His name. His name also represents a place of safety. In Proverbs 18:10, we read of this security: "The name of the LORD is a strong tower: the righteous run into it and are safe." His name exemplifies everything that He is: powerful, great, and excellent. His name speaks of His character, and it tells us who He is and what He can do. When we call on Him, everything that He is, shows up.

His name also signifies His authority. We can call on the owner of creation. His name defines Him as a powerful protector. The name of the Almighty reveals His attributes and accomplishments, by which He is made known. He is LORD. In its simplest form, LORD means owner. We identify Him as owner because of His works. He created the heavens and the earth. Although there may be those who ascribe His greatness to pagan deities, they cannot provide a shred of evidence that their god is the owner of the heaven and the earth and they are certainly not more powerful than the Creator God.

Proverbs 18 says that His name is like a strong tower that the righteous can run into for protection. When we cry out to Him in moments of despair, whatever we need in that space of time is represented in His name. We can call on Him and be confident in His strength and power to deliver us. In one situation, you may prepare yourself to enter His presence to worship Him. In the other, you are running to Him as a child would run to a father when he is afraid or hurt. It is the condition of your heart that He sees. He responds to your need for Him.

The book of Hebrews says we can come before the King confidently. When our hearts are upright before YAH, we are invited into the secret place. He bids us come.

> *Let us draw near with a true heart in full assurance of faith, having our hearts sprinkled from an evil conscience and our bodies washed with pure water (Hebrews 10:22 NKJV).*

We are encouraged to draw near and fellowship with Abba. Nevertheless, we should be mindful of how we present ourselves to the King of kings. Psalm 100:4 gives us the blueprint for how we are to present ourselves before Him.

> *Enter into His gates with thanksgiving, And into His courts with praise. Be thankful to Him, and bless His name (Psalm 100:4 NKJV).*

Another example is given in Exodus 21:12 when YHVH said to Moses, "Come up to Me". The phrase "come up to me" is reminiscent of a king granting a subject permission to come before him. The Most High allows us to come because we are in a relationship with Him. It is not because of anything good that we have done. It has everything to do with the finished work of Messiah, our kinsman-redeemer. The price has been paid for our sins and we have been given access to the

Holy of Holies. We know from the passage in the book of Hebrews that we can go before the throne boldly. If we were to restate this, it means that we can approach the throne with confidence. Yashua, our Redeemer paid the price for our sin so that we can have access to the throne of grace as sons of Elohim.

> *Let us therefore come boldly to the throne of grace, that we may obtain mercy and find grace to help in time of need (Hebrews 4:16 NKJV).*

There is still something extremely humbling about being able to come before the Creator of heaven and earth and we should never take that for granted. To enter with confidence does not mean we should bypass showing the respect that He is due. We are not to esteem the Most High lightly or address Him frivolously. The confidence being referred to in Hebrew 4:16, is the status restored to us as sons because the Lamb has been slain for our sin. In Messiah, we are complete, holy, righteous, and redeemed. Prior to salvation, we had to go to the priests to make atonement for us. The priests served as mediators. They made supplications on our behalf, but we could only go so far. We could not go into the Holy of Holies.

> *Therefore, brothers and sisters, since we have confidence to enter the Most Holy Place by the blood of Jesus, 20 by a new and living way opened for us through the curtain, that is, his body, 21 and since we have a great priest over the house of God, 22 let us draw near to God with a sincere heart and with the full assurance that faith brings, having our hearts sprinkled to cleanse us from a guilty conscience and having our bodies washed with pure water (Hebrews 10:19-22 NIV).*

The confidence we now have is grounded in the fact that the Messiah is our High Priest and His death, burial and resurrection made it possible for us to have access to the Father. We have been restored to the position that Adam had when he walked and talked with the Creator in the Garden of Eden. Yet, there is more to consider before entering His presence.

Traditionally, people have accepted that there is something distinctive about royalty. When we consider how things are done in present times, monarchs are held in the highest regard and treated with reverence and respect. There is a long list of protocols that guides one's behavior and interactions with royalty. If you were invited to meet the Queen of England, you would not just walk in, and say, "Hello." Certain protocol and etiquette must be observed before entering her presence. It is standard procedure to bow or curtsey. You would also need to address her as "Your Majesty "and present her with a gift.

Needless to say, you would not present yourself before the queen in a disheveled way. Those given the invitation to visit Buckingham Palace want to present themselves in a professional and refined manner. Wearing formal clothing would certainly be at the top of the list. If such formal protocol is used when meeting a mortal monarch here on earth, what should be considered when approaching the King of Kings? These are external things that we can do to make ourselves presentable, but we know that our Father is looking at our heart. By no means should we think that we must wait to dress in a certain manner or a certain posture in order to pray when we are in trouble. We can call out to YAH or pray at all times. Above all things, we need to honor Him for who He is. The heavenly Father deserves honor and respect and it is vitally important to remember this fact. He is worthy. We see in the verse below what the Highest thinks about His honor.

> *A son honors his father, and a servant his master. If then I am the Father, Where is My honor? And if I am a Master, Where is My reverence? Says the LORD of hosts to you priests who despise My name. Yet you say, 'In what way have we despised Your name?' (Malachi 1:6 NKJV)*

Humbling ourselves before the King is a great way to show honor to Him. Kneeling is just one way that symbolizes humility or bowing our heads when we pray. Philippians 2:10 tells us that at the name of the Messiah every knee will bow. What does it mean to bow the knee before Elohim? The bowing of the knee indicates a lowering of oneself to the One who is greater in power and authority. Kneeling and bowing is not mandatory every time you pray. They are outward appearances that do not tell the truth about the heart of the worshipper. Some may use this position to show submission to the Highest. However, submission and humility are not merely an outward show of submission; it should be an inward action that really connects, respects, and gives adoration to the giver of life. We know that He loves us, but we cannot forget who He is and the respect due for Him. He says this about Himself:

> *"For from the rising of the sun, even to its going down, My name shall be great among the Gentiles; In every place incense shall be offered to My name, And a pure offering; For My name shall be great among the nations, Says the Lord of hosts "* *(Malachi. 1:11, NKJV).*

Our Father deserves much more respect than a worldly sovereign, but do we even give Him that much? He deserves our utmost respect and devotion. In the natural, you would not go into the presence of a great king without a gift. It is no different for the supreme King. Psalm 95:2 tells us to come into His presence with thanksgiving. Our adoration and worship are our gifts to Him. The example shown to us in the book of Esther offer more insight into the way kings were esteemed during her day.

> *Now it happened on the third day that Esther put on her royal robes and stood in the inner court of the king's palace, across from the king's house, while the king sat on his royal throne in the royal house, facing the entrance of the house.*
> *2 So it was, when the king saw Queen Esther standing in the court, that she found favor in his sight, and the king held out to Esther the golden scepter that was in his hand. Then Esther went near and touched the top of the scepter (Esther 5:1-3, NKJV).*

Esther prepared herself by putting on her best attire and following the protocol of waiting in the inner court for the king to first recognize her and then bid her to come closer. Again, this does not mean that we need to be dressed in formal attire before praying. These are outward examples of how we should prepare our heart, mind, and soul when we pray. Obviously, there will be times when you cry out to the Father instantaneously because of distress or in a moment of crisis. He understands this, but also consider that when you cry out to Him in times of distress, you are fixing your heart, mind, and soul solely on Him. During those times, you come to Him because you recognize who He is, and you understand that He has the power to help you. You are not coming to Him dismissively.

Ways to Prepare Yourself

Entering the secret place during our time of prayer should be paramount for children of the Most High. That is the time to honor, praise and entreat Him. Most importantly, we should consider that when we enter the secret place, we are approaching the King of kings and LORD of Lords. Maintaining a posture of reverence is fitting when coming to the throne. As His children, we have been given the right to come near. There are various poses for prayer. Some may kneel, stand with head bowed, lay in a prostrate position, or sit. But before you begin speaking, you want to prepare yourself mentally and emotionally. Take time to think about who He is and all that He has done. By doing this, you will be moved to worship. You may also play praise and worship music softly or sing praises from your heart. These things help to set the atmosphere and get you ready for prayer. Just thinking about the sacrifice He made for you to receive salvation is more than enough to cause you to give Him thanks. This is a time to leave the cares of the world behind as you meditate on His goodness.

When you take the time to settle yourself and set your heart and mind on Him, you begin to sense a tugging in your spirit as if He is drawing you closer. He is beckoning you to draw near. There are also times when you will have a strong desire to praise Him and you may begin praying in your heavenly language. Think: (I am about to present myself to the Creator of the universe. He is the Almighty God. He is my heavenly Father, and He loves me). Reflect on His goodness. Remember the times He has brought you through a difficult situation. As you continue to meditate, praise, and honor Him, you will begin to feel a stirring in your heart. Sometimes you may weep or rejoice. As you continue to worship, you will feel a tugging in your soul that your Father is bidding you come.

Remember the words of Paul when he admonished us to present our bodies as a living sacrifice. You are the sacrifice, and you must die to your flesh daily. So there may be areas that the Holy Spirit points out to you that need correction. Agree with Him quickly, repent and continue in worship.

> *I beseech you therefore, brethren, by the mercies of God, that you present your bodies a living sacrifice, holy, acceptable to God, which is your reasonable service (Romans 12:1 NKJV).*

It will be important for you to stay focused. The enemy will try to bring all sorts of distractions. Try to minimize opportunities for distraction as best you can before you go into prayer. Focus on the Word and what He said while you pray. Do not focus on the problems. You should be laser-focused on maximizing your time with the Father as you listen for His instructions.

As you continue to meditate on His goodness and worship Him, spontaneous praise will begin to spring forth from your lips. Songs of worship may come to mind that cause you to clap or wave your hands. There are times when you are moved to dance or shout. The verse below tells us how to enter into the presence of the Highest.

> *Enter into His gates with thanksgiving, and into His courts with praise. Be thankful to Him, and bless His name (Psalm 100:4).*

You do not want to go before the Most High murmuring and complaining. As you worship and adore the Most High, you are preparing your altar and your worship is opening a portal with a direct connection to the throne room in heaven. Continue to worship as He draws you closer. Praise open doors, much like opening a portal that will give you access into the spirit realm. When we extol Him and glorify Him, we demonstrate our recognition of His rank and status as ruler and creator of all. He is deserving of glory so we must esteem Him highly. For some time, I have read and or sung Psalm 92 on the Sabbath day. The passage begins with the reminder to give thanks and to sing praises to His name.

> *It is good to give thanks to the Lord, and to sing praises to Your name, O Most High; to declare Your lovingkindness in the morning, and Your faithfulness every night (Psalm 92:1-2. NKJV).*

You will sense in your spirit that you are in the place of peace, rest, and blessed assurance. It is the dimension where the will of YHVH is manifested. It is here where you adore Him, fellowship with Him and make your requests known. Understand that worship will not be the same each time or the same for everyone.

Chapter 5

PRAYING IN THE SECRET PLACE

P rayer is the meeting place for the collaboration between heaven and earth. This is the place where believers commune and fellowship with the heavenly Father. Notice in the verse below that the Father is already in the secret place.

> *But you, when you pray, go into your room, and when you have shut your door, pray to your Father who is in the secret place; and your Father who sees in secret will reward you openly (Matthew 6:6 NKJV).*

The message being communicated by Messiah is that your time of prayer should not be a performance for others, to gain respect or appear righteous before men. Prayer is a time to connect with the Most High. The idea of going into a prayer closet is simply identifying a quiet place in which to pray regularly. The concept of going into your prayer closet can also be a reminder to look for a place where you will have little to no interruption. Messiah would often go to the mountain to pray. His secret place was not the bedroom closest. He chose a mountain. We also see in Matthew 14:23 that He would go alone.

> *And when He had sent the multitudes away, He went up on the mountain by Himself to pray. Now when evening came, He was alone there (Matthew 14:23 NKJV).*

If Messiah took time to pray and spend time with the Father concerning His will, why wouldn't we? As one would imagine, there had to be many things competing for His time and attention. Yet, He found it necessary to escape all the frenzy to be alone with the Most High. Messiah's alone time with the Almighty, to pray and to give Him his full attention is an indication of how important these times of prayer really are.

The Throne Room

Can you envision what it will be like to approach the throne of the Most High? We are referencing the King of kings, whose glory, reign, and power are above any other throne that ever existed or will ever exist. It may be difficult for us today because we were not born during the days when most nations were ruled by sovereigns. But to envision the King sitting on His throne surrounded by the angelic host is daunting. I imagine that one would immediately be filled with awe and reverence as they beheld His magnificence.

Though we may find it difficult to imagine how we would respond when standing before the actual throne of the Highest, we can gain some perspective from the testimony of those who did. The prophet Isaiah tells of his experience:

> *1 In the year that King Uzziah died, I saw the Lord sitting on a throne, high and lifted up, and the train of His robe filled the temple.*
> *2 Above it stood seraphim; each one had six wings: with two he covered his face, with two he covered his feet, and with two he flew.*
> *3 And one cried to another and said: "Holy, holy, holy is the Lord of hosts; The whole earth is full of His glory!"*

⁴And the posts of the door were shaken by the voice of him who cried out, and the house was filled with smoke.
⁵ So I said: "Woe is me, for I am undone! Because I am a man of unclean lips, And I dwell in the midst of a people of unclean lips; For my eyes have seen the King, The Lord of hosts." (Isaiah 6:1-5 NKJV).

The passage lets us know that when Isaiah entered the presence of YAH, he was quickly aware of his own sinfulness.

The prophet Ezekiel said his encounter caused him to fall on his face.

And above the firmament over their heads was the likeness of a throne, in appearance like a sapphire stone; on the likeness of the throne was a likeness with the appearance of a man high above it. 27 Also from the appearance of His waist and upward I saw, as it were, the color of amber with the appearance of fire all around within it; and from the appearance of His waist and downward I saw, as it were, the appearance of fire with brightness all around. 28 Like the appearance of a rainbow in a cloud on a rainy day, so was the appearance of the brightness all around it. This was the appearance of the likeness of the glory of the Lord. So when I saw it, I fell on my face, and I heard a voice of One speaking (Ezekiel 1:26-28 NKJV).

Both prophets knew that they were in the presence of excellence and great power. They responded with reverence. As believers and children of the Highest, we also have access to the throne room. Through our eternal High Priest who has made atonement for our sin, we can approach the throne boldly! But when presented with an opportunity to come before a King, we are to bring a gift (Ps. 45:11,12). We find in Hebrew 13:15 that the gift we are to bring is our sacrifice of praise.

The Key of David

The key of David was praise and worship. The Most High inhabits the praise of His people, which means that He dwells in that atmosphere. Praise and worship are spiritual keys in the kingdom to help you unlock doors in the heavenly realm. During your time of worship, you are creating a portal that gives you access to the heavenly realm. The key of David appears only twice in the Bible. The first time it appears is in Isaiah where it states:

> *The key of the house of David I will lay on his shoulder; So he shall open, and no one shall shut; And he shall shut, and no one shall open (Isaiah 22:22 NKJV).*

The second occurrence is found in the Book of Revelation.

> *And to the angel of the church in Philadelphia write, 'These things says He who is holy, He who is true, "He who has the key of David, He who opens and no one shuts, and shuts and no one opens" (Revelation 3:7 NKJV).*

In the Old Testament, the Hebrew word for "key" (in the phrase, "key of the house of David"), is "maphteach" It is defined by Young's Analytical Concordance of the Bible, as, "key, opener" or "opening." Basically, a key is used to lock or unlock a door. To look at it another way, we use keys to gain access to things that have been locked away or we use them to prevent others from things they do not have a right to. These keys allow the people of the Most High to unlock doors in the Kingdom and enable them to rule with dominion and the authority given to us by the Messiah.

And I will give you the keys of the kingdom of heaven, and whatever you bind on earth will be bound in heaven, and whatever you loose on earth will be loosed in heaven." (Matthew 16:19 NKJV).

The key of the house of David combines the anointings of priests and kings to rule on earth. This was the original intent of the Creator. He created man to rule on earth and have dominion. To bind and to lose simply means to forbid by an indisputable authority and to permit by an indisputable authority ('Binding and Loosing').

It is very important for us to understand how these keys work in the spirit realm. Keys can be used to lock a door and it is also used to unlock it. Notice that Messiah said keys, indicating that we are given more than one. Consider that these spiritual keys can be used to give us access to knowledge concerning spiritual things. One of the greatest ways to revolutionize your prayer life is to begin with songs of praise and words of adoration. You should not begin by asking the Father for things. Remember, He already knows what things you need. Sometimes your prayer will begin spontaneously because of your praise. Praise is a weapon. When you worship and praise on earth, you are creating a portal to connect YAH's heavenly kingdom to your location here on earth. During your time of praise and worship, doors are opened to you to receive revelation from heaven. Knowing this, it is understandable why Satan hates praise and worship. It drives him away. Remember how the demon spirit left Saul when David began playing his instrument. Also, think about how the Israelites would enter battle by sending the singers first. This lets you know that worship is a powerful weapon.

Armed with this knowledge, it should transform your prayer life. During your time of communing with King, you come into agreement with Him concerning things you are to "bind" or forbid and those things you are to "loose" or permit. Be sure to take advantage of these secret weapons. Use them to destroy the strongholds of the enemy. The forces of evil will do anything to stop believers from praying. Your goal is to pray without demonic interference.

There are times when the Holy Spirit also enables believers to engage with the unseen realm as we pray in heavenly language. As you continue to offer up praise and thanksgiving, you may begin to weep or sing in this language. It is not uncommon for the Holy Spirit to prompt you to pray about certain things or for certain people during this time. You may be prompted to pray about certain situations or for certain people or be compelled to pray for the body of Christ, religious leaders, your family and friends, the nation of Israel, and others. Additionally, He will begin to show you things to pray about in your own life. It would appear that these are keys to knowledge or spiritual insight into things to come. As sons of the Most High, our primary role is to bring the order of heaven to earth like the Messiah said in Matthew 6:10. He told us to pray for the Father's will to be done on earth as it is heaven. Pray using the Scriptures to guide you. When we pray, we are engaging another dimension. Paul tells us in Ephesians 6:12 that we are warring against principalities in high places.

Pray Effectively

The Scriptures tell us that men are to pray always. Yet, we see that some prayers will not be heard. It goes without saying that if we are going to pray, it should be our desire to have our prayers answered. Are there times when a prayer is ineffective? James 5:16 tells us that the effectual fervent prayer of a righteous man avails much. So then, there are times when prayer can be ineffective. The Book of James also specifies why some prayers are ineffective.

> *"You ask and do not receive, because you ask wrongly, to spend it on your passions." (James 4:3 ESV).*

In addition, Psalm 66:18 tells us that iniquity in our heart will also prevent our prayers from being heard. Could this be why the disciples asked the Messiah to teach them how to pray? If we are going to spend time in prayer, we want to be assured that Abba YAH will hear us and grant our requests. It is also important to know that all prayers are not the same nor is one type of prayer more important than another.

As a believer in a relationship with the Highest, we must pray. Prayer is the means of talking to Him, just as we talk to our family members and friends. Many believers engage in various forms of prayer, but are they always effective and fervent?

One of the most effective forms of prayer is to pray the word! Repeat what YAH has already said concerning you, your situation, and His people. Recite His word back to Him. It represents agreement. He invites us to put Him in remembrance of His promises. As you pray and remind Him of the promises He made, also thank Him for being faithful to His word.

> ***Put me in remembrance: let us plead together: declare thou, that thou mayest be justified (Isaiah 43:26 KJV).***

As you continue praying the Word, you are coming into agreement with the proclamations of the King in the spirit realm. The angels move at His word. Your confessions also cause demons to tremble. The words you use during prayer are doing something. They are creative forces. With words, Elohim created the heavens and the earth. When He speaks the Word into your heart, you are to speak it back to Him. It should flow from Him into you and then out of you. Our Father's word has great power, and He has given that power to us. We are told in Proverbs 18:21 that the power of death and life is in our tongue.

Chapter 6

VARIOUS TYPES OF PRAYER

Growing up in the church provided me with many opportunities to engage in prayer and observe those who prayed. During a traditional church service, we were accustomed to the opening prayers used at the beginning of the service; the prayer over the offering and the benediction to end the service. It was also common for pastors or guest speakers to pray before delivering the sermon. I have also attended churches where a special time of prayer was set for the congregation to come together and pray for the church, those in need of healing, its leaders, specific requests, and the body of Christ.

For years, I viewed prayer as a one-way street. My personal time of prayer normally began with words of thanks to the Father for allowing me to see another day. I then prayed for specific needs for myself, or others and I ended my prayer by saying "in Jesus' name, Amen." It did not enter my mind that the One I was praying to might also have something to say to me. After the prayer ended, I was off to do other things. However, it has only been within the last 20 or so years that I began learning about the ways in which we pray.

We should consider the question that the disciples asked Messiah in Luke 11, "Lord, teach us to pray." These men had walked with Messiah for three years, listening to Him and observing Him.

However, they realized that there was something special about His prayer life that was missing from theirs. He did not respond in a way that would lead us to believe that the disciples had asked an absurd question. Yahshua answered their request with specific instructions in this version of what is called, The Lord's Prayer found in Matthew 6:9-15:

> *After this manner therefore pray ye:*
>
> *Our Father which art in heaven, Hallowed be thy name.*
>
> *10 Thy kingdom come, Thy will be done in earth, as it is in heaven.*
>
> *11 Give us this day our daily bread.*
>
> *12 And forgive us our debts, as we forgive our debtors.*
>
> *13 And lead us not into temptation, but deliver us from evil: For thine is the kingdom, and the power, and the glory, for ever. Amen. (KJV).*

Just like the disciples, we too must learn how to pray. Notice that Messiah could have told the disciples to start by praying, "Dear God," but instead, He told them to begin by saying, "Our Father," They were taught to begin by acknowledging who the Father is and then to give honor to His name. In the following verses, we see that Yashua began His prayers in the same manner.

> *And He went a little beyond them, and fell on His face and prayed, saying, "My Father, if it is possible, let this cup pass from Me; yet not as I will, but as You will" (Matthew 26:39 NASB).*

He went away again a second time and prayed, saying, "My Father, if this cup cannot pass away unless I drink it, Your will be done" (Matthew 26:42 NASB).

So they took away the stone. Then Jesus looked up and said, "Father, I thank You that You have heard Me (John 11:41 NIV).

After Jesus said this, He looked toward heaven and prayed: "Father, the hour has come. Glorify Your Son, that Your Son may glorify You (John 17:1 NIV).

In the same way, we are to approach the Creator of the Universe as our loving Father, but with reverence. These examples reveal the connection we have with the Almighty. We are born into His family.

"But as many as received Him, to them He gave the right to become children of God, to those who believe in His name" (John 1:12 NASB).

The next step is to recognize that He is sovereign, the owner of the heavens and earth. He is king and He has a kingdom. The prayer in Matthew 6 teaches us that the Most High is the Highest of all, and we are to submit to His authority. When we fully understand that during our time of prayer, we are communing with the One who reigns over everything that exists, it should come as no surprise that we are told not to worry about what we should eat or drink or what we should wear. He is the king and owner over of all things, after all. By saying, "Give us this day our daily bread," we are admitting that we are not independent of Him. This is an admission that we need Him to provide for our basic needs as a good father provides for his children.

Types of Prayer

There are many types of prayers, and we find evidence of this in the Scripture. Prayers can be motivated by different things. For example, some prayers may be motivated by a need for healing, deliverance, financial need, sorrow, or a grateful heart. Other prayers may be the result of our desire to fellowship with and commune with the Most High. Whatever the reason, it is important to make prayer a priority. It is our lifeline to the kingdom of heaven, and it is our way to fellowship with Abba YAH and develop a personal relationship with Him.

Travailing Prayer

There are various types of prayers in Scripture. We should be cautious of all who tell us that there is one specific way to commune with Elohim. There may be times when we are led to intercede on behalf of others, make supplications or travail in prayer like Messiah did in the Garden of Gethsemane. The word travail is the same word used for labor pains when giving birth to a child. It is an intense time of prayer when the Holy Spirit is praying through us with groanings.

> *Likewise the Spirit also helps in our weaknesses. For we do not know what we should pray for as we ought, but the Spirit Himself makes intercession for us with groanings which cannot be uttered. 27 Now He who searches the hearts knows what the mind of the Spirit is, because He makes intercession for the saints according to the will of God (Romans 8:26-27 NKJV).*

Travailing prayer is the most intense type of prayer for a believer. There is usually a burden that comes upon you to cause you to cry out in desperation or it may be caused because of sorrow that evokes this deep, sorrowful type of prayer. Travail births something in the earth. Isaiah 66:8 says, "…for as soon as Zion travailed, she brought forth her children." There is also the way Job prayed during his time of suffering. He was moved to cry out for a mediator between man and the Almighty because he had no explanation for his severe tests. I believe his prayer helped to bring for the Messiah – our mediator.

Paul also travailed in prayer. He says in Galatians 4:19, "My little children, of whom I travail in birth again until Christ be formed in you".

Intercessory Prayer

Prayer can be used for the several ways we communicate with the heavenly Father, but there is another level of prayer that invokes our love and compassion to cry out on behalf of others. It involves sacrificing our time to commune with the Almighty about things that may not necessarily concern us. This is intercessory prayer – the sacrifice of our time to enter the throne room of the sovereign King on behalf of another person, people group, situation, church, or community. Intercession is an example of the second great commandment to love your neighbor as you love yourself.

In Exodus 32:11-14, there is a record of a remarkable prayer of intercession. It is the prayer of Moses' appeal to the Most High not to destroy Israel for their idolatry. The Bible describes him as being a humble man, but he was also an intercessor. Moses was given the special task of going before Pharaoh as the spokesperson for the God of the children of Israel with a simple message, "Let My people go!"

The exodus from the land of Egypt came as the result of many miraculous signs and terrible plagues that ultimately forced Pharaoh to submit to the will of the one true God. However, it was not long after the Israelites witnessed these mighty events and the awe-inspiring moment of hearing the voice of the Highest speak to Moses from the clouds as described in Exodus 19:9, "Behold, I come to you in the thick cloud, that the people may hear when I speak with you", that the people sinned greatly. Before Moses could come down from the mountain, the people began worshipping a golden calf.

It may be hard for us to imagine how the people could resort to such idolatry and paganism in such a short time, but it is equally amazing how Moses interceded for them. In Exodus 32:30, Moses told the people he would go up unto the LORD to try to make atonement for their sin. This example of selflessness saved the lives of many of the children of Israel and kept them from the wrath of YHVH. This would be one of many prayers of intercession offered up by Moses on behalf of Israel. At times, their behavior begged for judgment, but Moses cared enough to stand in the gap for them. May we be reminded of this act of unselfishness in our day. One of the highest acts of supplication is to pray and intercede on behalf of others when we pray, even when we feel that they are undeserving.

Another great intercessor was Nehemiah. He was agonized by the dismal report brought to him concerning the ruined walls of Jerusalem. He was broken-hearted after learning of the ruined walls, the desolate temple, and the burned gates. But what caused him even more pain was the thought of the holy name of the Most High being ridiculed by the heathens. So, Nehemiah began to intercede.

> *⁴ So it was, when I heard these words, that I sat down and wept, and mourned for many days; I was fasting and praying before the God of heaven.*
> *⁵ And I said: "I pray, Lord God of heaven, O great and awesome God, You who keep Your covenant and mercy with those who love [c]You and observe [d]Your commandments, 6 please let Your ear be attentive and Your eyes open, that You may hear the prayer of Your servant which I pray before You now, day and night, for the children of Israel Your servants, and confess the sins of the children of Israel which we have sinned against You. Both my father's house and I have sinned. 7 We have acted very corruptly against You, and have not kept the commandments, the statutes, nor the ordinances which You commanded Your servant Moses. 8 Remember, I pray, the word that You commanded Your servant Moses, saying, 'If you [e]are unfaithful, I will scatter you among the nations; 9 but if you return to Me, and keep My commandments and do them, though some of you were cast out to the farthest part of the heavens, yet I will gather them from there, and bring them to the place which I have chosen as a dwelling for My name.' 10 Now these are Your servants and Your people, whom You have redeemed by Your great power, and by Your strong hand (Nehemiah 1:4-10 NKJV).*

In the book of John 17:9, we also see the Messiah interceding for others. He said, "I pray for them. I am not praying for the world, but for those You have given me, for they are Yours." He also interceded for Peter. In Luke 22:32, he says to Peter, "But I have prayed for thee, that thy faith fail not: and when thou art converted, strengthen thy brethren." How much better our world would be if we found time to pray more for others as much as we pray for ourselves.

Intimate prayer

The door that leads to the secret place opens during intimate prayer. During this type of prayer, you just want to be in His presence. You leave the cares of the world behind in fellowship with Him and just offer up prayers of adoration and praise. It is not uncommon for you to be prompted to this time of prayer during the early morning or to be awakened from sleep. You are usually given a gentle nudge and sense a tugging in your soul to pray. It is easy to lose track of time as the weight of the world is lifted from your shoulders and you find rest for your weary soul. You get lost in worship and experience a level of intimacy that leaves you speechless and you will never find enough words to give Him thanks just for who He is.

Times of intimacy with the Most High is a time when deep calls out to deep and you know that He is there with you. Your mind, body and soul enter rest. This is a place where the weary cease from troubling and the weak say that I am strong. You cry Abba and you know that He hears you. There is no other place you would rather be. This is the secret place. A place of communion. A place of complete surrender and intimacy – this is the place where YAH dwells. The place where you long to be because it is so sweet, so perfect, and safe.

Prayers to Avoid

Ritualistic prayer – This type of prayer seems very prescriptive, very much like the prayer we say over a meal or an opening prayer for an event. Oftentimes, the words are rehearsed repeatedly until it is mere rote memorization. During these times, we believe that the most important thing is to say the right words.

Prayer of convenience – With this type of prayer, it is like fulfilling a duty or checking something off the checklist. To impress ourselves or others, we say that we pray every day. It is done almost out of habit or as an act of self-righteousness because we believe the Most High is keeping a scorecard to see how often we pray. We believe that the Father will be moved by our dutifulness to pray, and He will look kindly on us.

Know that your times of prayer will be transformed if you would see prayer as a time of fellowship and communion with your heavenly Father. He is not there just to listen to you. He wants to respond and oftentimes, His response is the answer to your specific prayer or things He wants you to do.

The prayers mentioned are just a few of the various types of ways to pray to our Creator. Yet, there are times when He simply wants to speak to us during this set-apart time. Before you end your prayer, take some time to listen. Be silent before Him for a few minutes and just listen to see if He wants to say something back to you. He may give you specific strategies concerning an issue that you are dealing with. He may also bring a verse of Scripture to mind. If He does, read it and meditate on it. Be careful to listen for new instructions. There may be times when you are given a vision of things to come either during your time of active prayer or as you wait in His presence. This is a time when the cares of the world seem trivial and small. Your spirit man will be refreshed, and you leave knowing that all is well.

A word of caution, you should never get locked into thinking that the Holy Spirit will move the exact same way every time when you pray. When you do that, you run the risk of being ritualistic. When you sense the Spirit lifting, end your prayer with thanksgiving. If He spoke to you, get into the habit of writing the messages in a journal. Rereading those words months and years later will cause you to continually value and appreciate YAH's goodness.

Chapter 7

A MODEL PRAYER

Daniel's Example

In the following verses, you will find portions of Daniel's prayer. His prayer comes as the result of reading the words of the prophet Jeremiah (Dan. 9:1–3). As Daniel reads the writings of Jeremiah referencing Jerusalem's desolation that lasted seventy years, he is moved to offer up prayers for his people. Yet again, Israel is needing to be rescued from the lands of her oppressors and the Babylonian system. The children of Israel find themselves in a similar situation today. As descendants of the children of Israel, we acknowledge the truth about who we are as a people and see how far we have fallen from our rightful place as the chosen people, Daniel models for us the attitude we are to have as we petition the Most High. Like Daniel, we are to pray for the restoration of Israel to their land.

This prayer for the nation of Israel can be found in the book of Daniel 9. Without a doubt, a life of prayer was not a new thing for Daniel; as Daniel 6 indicates, his practice of praying three times a day towards Jerusalem was a regular and established habit. Notice that He begins the prayer by glorifying the Most High. He extols Him and calls Him great and awesome. Daniel declares the attributes of YAH depicting Him as being merciful and a keeper of covenants. These words indicate that Daniel is aware of these passages from the Torah, and he agrees with those descriptions. What is key in these verses, is that Daniel does not immediately begin his prayer with petitions. He comes before the Most High with adoration and an acknowledgment of who He is as the great I AM.

Next, we see that Daniel acknowledges the known sins. He says that we have sinned and committed iniquity. We may wonder why he includes himself in admitting sin, but it is important to know that YAH sees the nation of Israel as one nation. They are His people. Daniel may have lived uprightly, but the plight of the nation also affected him. He was taken into slavery along with others who may have gone astray by committing iniquity. Daniel says that the nation was guilty of doing wicked things and that they were also rebellious.

> **And I prayed to the Lord my God, and made confession, and said, "O Lord, great and awesome God, who keeps His covenant and mercy with those who love Him, and with those who keep His commandments, 5 we have sinned and committed iniquity, we have done wickedly and rebelled, even by departing from Your precepts and Your judgments (Daniel 9:4-5 NKJV).**

Daniel continues confessing the sins of the nation and says that all Israel has transgressed the laws of YAH. This is also our plight. We failed to obey His laws, statutes, and commandments. As a result, the wrath of the Almighty was poured out on us and we find ourselves living in the lands of our captivities.

> *Yes, all Israel has transgressed Your law, and has departed so as not to obey Your voice; therefore the curse and the oath written in the Law of Moses the servant of God have been poured out on us, because we have sinned against Him (Daniel 9:11 NKJV).*

After Daniel confessed the sins of his people, he begins to recite all the good things that the Most High had done for Israel. He acknowledged how YAH had brought the people out of Egypt with a mighty hand, then he begins his petition. Daniel showed reverence for the Almighty first before asking for anything. What is interesting is that he does not ask for his wants or needs to be met, he intercedes for his people. Daniel did not purely pray for his own comfort and protection during this period of enslavement. His concern was to pray for YAH's people and His kingdom.

Daniel prays on behalf of his people because the time is drawing near to the completion of the years of captivity. Yet, he does not see a nationwide change in the hearts of Israel. This lack of contrition may have caused the prophet to grieve even more during his time of intercession.

> *As it is written in the Law of Moses, all this disaster has come upon us; yet we have not made our prayer before the Lord our God, that we might turn from our iniquities and understand Your truth (Daniel 9:13 NKJV).*

Like Daniel, so too are we to confess the sins of our people and acknowledge the justice of YAH's judgment. Our punishment was severe, but we were not utterly destroyed. Daniel did not make excuses for Israel or question the fairness of the Most High's dealings with them nor can we. We fully deserved the outcome we have experienced for our rebellion against our gracious and loving Father. But like Daniel, we can ask for the anger of the Almighty to be turned away. As descendants of the children of Israel, we must humble ourselves and make no excuses for our wickedness. In verses 17-19, we see Daniel's humility. He beseeched the Father to hear the prayer and see the desolation of His people not because of Daniel's righteousness, but for the Most High's sake.

> *Now therefore, our God, hear the prayer of Your servant, and his supplications, and for the Lord's sake [a]cause Your face to shine on [b]Your sanctuary, which is desolate. 18 O my God, incline Your ear and hear; open Your eyes and see our desolations, and the city which is called by Your name; for we do not present our supplications before You because of our righteous deeds, but because of Your great mercies. 19 O Lord, hear! O Lord, forgive! O Lord, listen and act! Do not delay for Your own sake, my God, for Your city and Your people are called by Your name"(Daniel 9: 17-19 NKJV).*

We too can beseech YAH on behalf of our nation, it is vitally important to remember that He has promised to restore His people, but not because we are so good. He said He would do it for His sake. He is protecting His name. Like Daniel, we should be moved to pray unceasingly, that the Most High would do what He has promised concerning His people.

The Book of Deuteronomy spoke not only of the judgment that was to come on the nation of Israel because of their disobedience against the Most High, it also told of the promise of redemption. Things change in our favor, and we are restored when we repent of the sins and turn to YAH in the places where He has scattered us. The Most High promised to restore our fortunes and gather us once again to our land (Deut. 30:2–3).

Daniel prayed for this in his prayer. He asked that Abba YAH would hear the prayer of His servant, and his supplications, and for the Lord's sake cause His face to shine on His sanctuary, which is desolate, bringing the exile to an end (Dan. 9:17). It should be the earnest prayer of the children of Israel to be delivered from the land of captivity. We must intercede on behalf of those who show no penitence for our plight. They may not be moved to pray, but we can. It is not YAH's will for Israel to perish in exile.

The restoration of the children of Israel will bring glory to the holy King. The nations would see His mighty power like they did when he brought Israel out of Egypt. To show the greatness of His mercy and to exonerate the honor of His name, the Most High must once again restore His people and return them to the land of promise. So, Daniel prayed with boldness and confidence that YAH would hear his prayer and remember His promises concerning Israel. Let's follow his example by using his prayer as a model to petition our Father for favor and the restoration of His people as He promised our forefathers.

WORKS CITED

'Bible Map: Naioth (Mizpah 3)'. *Bible Atlas*,
https://bibleatlas.org/naioth.htm. Accessed 24 May 2022.

'Binding and Loosing'. *Wikipedia*, 27 Apr. 2022,
https://en.wikipedia.org/w/index.php?title=Binding_and_loosing&oldid=
1084910056.

'H3427 - Yāšaḇ - Strong's Hebrew Lexicon (Kjv)'. *Blue*
Letter Bible, https://www.blueletterbible.org/kjv/gen/1/1/s_1001.
Accessed 24 May 2022.

Hirsch, Emil G., and Immanuel Benzinger. 'SHIELD'.
Jewish Encyclopedia, https://www.jewishencyclopedia.com/articles/3791-
buckler. Accessed 24 May 2022.

Homan, John D. '"Soldier's Prayer": Heartfelt Bandanas
Presented to Local Troops"'. *The Southern Illinoisian*, 28 Jan. 2005,
https://thesouthern.com/news/local/soldiers-prayer-heartfelt-bandanas-
presented-to-local-troops/article_610e89a4-eddc-50a9-9fba-
300412801dc0.html.

The Editors of Encyclopaedia Britannica. 'Yahweh'.
Encyclopedia Britannica, 30 June 2021,
https://www.britannica.com/topic/Yahweh.

Notes

_____

_____

_____

_____

_____

_____

_____

_____

_____

_____

_____

_____

_____

_____

_____

_____

_____

_____

_____

_____

_____

_____

_____

_____

Made in the USA
Las Vegas, NV
03 September 2022

54624511R00037